All of us are called to realize the ...
blessing of our ability to enter into heartfelt dialogue
with the Lord and thus become pilgrims of hope."

Pope Francis has declared 2025 the Jubilee Year of
Hope, asking all Christians to "be passionate about
life and commit ourselves to caring lovingly for
those around us in every place where we live."

When the news is depressing, when our families
are fractured, when all prospects look bleak, that,
says Pope Francis, is when we need to pay care-
ful attention to *hope*, the fundamental virtue that
informs who we are as Catholic Christians.

As always, the pope's message is clear and strong.
We are called to be "pilgrims of hope and builders of
peace," basing our lives on Christ's resurrection. And
reflecting on the gospel message is where we find the
strength to be joyful in hope.

Here are thirty days of reflections based on Pope
Francis' words on hope. May they inspire and
strengthen you so that you may become a hope-filled
prophet of joy!

The quotes from Pope Francis
were chosen by Deborah McCann,
who also wrote the reflections
and the "Ponder" and "Pray" pieces.

The Jubilee Year of Hope logo was designed by Giacomo Travisani.
Copyright © Dicastery for Evangelization, Vatican City. All rights reserved.

Third Printing 2025

Copyright © 2017, 2024 **TWENTY-THIRD PUBLICATIONS**,
a division of Bayard; 977 Hartford Turnpike Unit A, Waterford, CT 06385;
860-437-3012 or 800-321-0411; twentythirdpublications.com.

Cover photo: M.MIGLIORATO/CPP/CIRIC

ISBN: 978-1-62785-258-6 ■ Printed in the U.S.A.

1 | LOOKING BEYOND THE NOW

*They who proclaim the hope of Jesus carry joy,
and they see a great distance because they know how
to see beyond evil and beyond their problems.*

I'm sure many of us are familiar with the phrase, "Been down so long it looks like up to me." Especially in times of personal or national or spiritual darkness, hope can be a very elusive virtue. We know faith is a gift, and we have guidelines for how to model charity, but hope can escape us. Pope Francis tells us not to worry. We are not meant to be prophets of doom but people who can see beyond the current situation to trust in the plans God has in mind. If we pause to consider God's hope in *us*, we may find hoping easier.

PONDER
Am I a hopeful person, or do I often fall into despondency?

PRAY
God of hope, remove any darkness that surrounds me, so that I may see you better!

2 | GOD IS WITH US

Jesus is always walking beside us, even in the darkest moments, and he will reveal his presence.

Pope Francis speaks of the disciples on the road to Emmaus as an example of how well Jesus understands our human propensities. The disciples are complaining that all their hopes are dashed with Jesus' death, that hope is lost, and that there's no sense in going on. What does Jesus do? First, says Pope Francis, he is patient. He listens, and then he begins to teach them, to remind them of how God has been working in history throughout all of time. In our darkest days and times, when we remember that God is present, then the light of hope can begin to shine in our hearts and help us to see.

PONDER
How often do I not see the forest of God's love for the trees of my own blindness?

PRAY
God of hope, walk with me and open my eyes to joy!

3 | NOURISHING THE ROOTS OF HOPE

*Hope is a gift from God. We must ask for it,
so that its light may shine on our darkness.*

"There is no corner of our heart that cannot be touched by God's love," says Pope Francis. Those are pretty encouraging words! When we make mistakes, God is there, never wavering in love. If we open ourselves to trusting in God's presence in our lives and in our world, we may begin to find the depths of hope buried within us and start to find the strength and conviction that comes from knowing that God is with us. This gift is already within us—we just have to help it grow.

PONDER

When was the last time I truly believed in God's unconditional love for me?

PRAY

God of hope, help me to watch for you, listen for you, and find you in the smallest moments of every day!

4 | THE HUMILITY OF HOPE

Hope is the humblest of virtues,
because it hides itself in this life.

When circumstances and situations threaten to defeat us, when we have lost our bearings and wonder what sense there is in action of any kind, Pope Francis reminds us of the remarkably resilient power of hope. It's not something outside of us, he says, but it hides within our life. It is something we carry in us, and it's up to us to pray to have it revealed so that we can share it with others. This small flame can become a vibrant blaze if we permit ourselves to trust in how God is working in each of us. How confident can we let ourselves be?

PONDER

Have I ever considered that I carry the seeds of hope within me?

PRAY

God of hope, help me to find the hope that's in me, so that I may help it grow.

5 | HOPE IS RISKY

Hope is a virtue of eager longing for the revelation of the Son of God; hope means striving toward this revelation, toward this joy.

Pope Francis consistently relates hope to joy. In his wisdom, he replaces words like anger, fear, and distrust with "eager longing," "striving," "deliverance." He is challenging us to change our focus, to leave ourselves open in faith, to act "as if," to believe that hope is possible. In dark times it's hard to imagine our "hearts filled with laughter" and our "tongues with joy," but hope will give us the tools to do just that—if we are ready to take that risk. And when we have once pushed that dark curtain aside, it will be hard to close it completely again!

PONDER
Am I ready to take the risk of living with hope?

PRAY
God of hope, help me find joy at least once today, and help me encourage others to find joy too.

6 | WE ARE NOT ALONE

God, who placed a sense of expectation within us,
waits patiently, even in the face of human corruption.
God never gives up.

When we have trouble being hopeful, Pope Francis says we should think of God's own hopefulness. Imagine for a moment God's undying hope for us in all our human frailty and our unfailing headlong dash down the wrong path. In spite of it all, God has such confidence in us that he continues to hope beyond hope—long beyond the limit where we would have given up. If God can be that hopeful about us, Pope Francis asks, can't we try to trust the hope inside us? What better companion could we have than one who understands us so completely!

PONDER
Does thinking of God's trust in me help me find courage? Or does it make me want to hide?

PRAY
God of hope, help me to trust in your presence, in your guidance, and in your love.

7 | ICON OF HOPE: LABOR

We are waiting, as a mother in childbirth.
This is truly a kind of labor.

Pope Francis is very fond of the image of a woman in labor to illustrate how we might recognize and embrace hope in our lives. At this moment of intense pain, a new life enters the world—and in the newborn child rest all the hopes and dreams of the parents. Just as a baby must emerge from inside its mother, so hope, hidden within us, must come forth through our labor. Once it is in the world, then we must continue to raise and nourish it so that all may reap its benefits.

PONDER

Have there been times in my life when I truly struggled to find hope?

PRAY

God of hope, remind me that everything worthwhile carries an element of struggle and pain. Help me trust in the journey.

8 | ICON OF HOPE: ANCHOR

*Where are we anchored? If we are settled where
everything is comfortable and secure,
then this is not hope.*

Early Christians used the symbol of the anchor to
represent their hope in God. Pope Francis asks us
to contemplate this image—do we cast the anchor
wide, trusting that it will pull us closer to the future
God wants us to build, or do we drop it closer to
where we are, where everything is well known and
safe? If we are content with, as Pope Francis says, "an
artificial lagoon" of our own making, without any
kind of risk of discovery, then we do not have hope.
Hope asks us to take a leap into the unknown, confident that God will guide us and not lead us astray.
How easy is that to do?

PONDER

Is God my anchor, my guide? Do I fully trust in
God's goodness and love?

PRAY

God of hope, help me to cast my anchor blindly,
knowing that you will bring me safely home.

9 | DISCOURAGEMENT IS EASY

*Reality is grim: there are so many people
who are suffering, so many wars, so much hate,
so much envy, so much spiritual worldliness,
and so much corruption.*

It's very easy to ponder hope in the abstract, but often holding hope up to the world seems foolhardy at best. It's easy, Pope Francis says, in the real world to be discouraged. That is why we have to remember that this gift of hope isn't something we should keep to ourselves—and it is just as real as the reality around us. Like all of God's gifts, it is meant to be shared, so that the light of hope may shine on others and help us all to find the voice we need to support the poor, the voiceless, the needy, and the fearful.

PONDER

Am I prone to discouragement and a sense of uselessness? How can I hold on to my hope?

PRAY

God of hope, keep reminding me of the strength of your hope in me, so that I may share the light of that hope always.

10 | HOPE CHANGES US

*We should ask for the grace to be
men and women of hope.*

Whether it's a change of job, or boss, or city, or a full house becoming an empty nest, or a change in elected officials, change itself is always difficult. Even when we look to embrace change as the right thing at the right time, it can be hard to adjust, filling us with uncertainty and fear. Pope Francis urges us not to be afraid of the ways hope can and will change us. He says we need to ask for the grace to be people of hope, people filled with light, who can help shine light into the dark spaces around us. Walking into the new reality secure in the knowledge that God is with us can make all the difference in how we respond—and in the effect we'll have on others.

PONDER

When have I feared a major change and then found it to be wonderful?

PRAY

God of hope, remove my fear and fill me with joy!

11 | HOPE VS. OPTIMISM

Don't confuse optimism with hope.
Optimism is a psychological attitude toward life.
Hope is also theological: God is there too.

Pope Francis reminds us that hope is different from an optimistic attitude. Optimism can be dashed when things don't go the way we expect, when we receive bad news, or when we don't get our way. Hope, on the other hand, exists in spite of negative outcomes, because God is the author of our hope. When hope is deeply rooted in our being, even the most dismal of prospects can be infused with possibility, because the truly hopeful, hope-filled person knows that he or she is not facing this journey alone.

PONDER

When have I found hope in the midst of grief?

PRAY

God of hope, remind me always of the psalmist who didn't fear the "valley of death," and fill me with that confidence and peace.

12 | THE GIFT OF HOPE

*The Lord consoles us and refashions us in hope
so that we might continue on.*

"When God closes a door, praise God in the hallway!" This sentiment is quite close to what Pope Francis is trying to tell us here. There are many times in life when we feel our prayers are not answered, when we are disappointed, discouraged, and afraid. Life can and does throw us curves that are hard to surmount. Sometimes it's hard to find God in these times, and sometimes it's easier to reject God as uncaring and uninvolved. Instead, Pope Francis says, call on God! God will always open a door for us. If we trust even in our darkness that God is working for good in our lives, then hope is alive in us. God is ready to help.

PONDER

When have I felt the presence or absence of God?

PRAY

God of hope, help me always to see the open door or the hallway of promise instead of the blank wall!

13 | THE JOY HOPE BRINGS

*Always ask God that we may be firmly founded
on the rock that is Jesus himself. He is our hope.*

When we place our trust and hope in transitory
things—material goods, "here today, gone tomorrow" things—Pope Francis says that we are missing
the most foundational thing of all. God is always
there, waiting for us, watching over us, ready to repay
our trust in him by filling us with joyous hope. This,
Pope Francis says, is true Christian joy: to be assured
of God's unconditional love and forgiveness, which
lead us to peace and joy. Too often in our world it's
easier to give in to despair than to rely on hope. But,
as the apostle Paul says, if God is for us (and God is),
who can be against us?

PONDER

Do I trust that God loves me, forgives me, and
wants me to live in joy?

PRAY

God of hope, trust does not come easily to me.
Open my heart to your presence.

14 | FAITH GIVES US HOPE

We gain victory over the world by our faith:
confessing it, nourishing it, and trusting in God.

Hope does not exist in a vacuum, Pope Francis reminds us. In fact, the three cardinal virtues of faith, hope, and love all work together. Faith reinforces hope and can keep us going when hope seems dim. Hope can increase our faith when we have trouble believing. Love works with both, because it is when we love that both faith and hope are renewed. All of these gifts are given us to share—and it's when we share them in trusting obedience to God that we can see how they are working in others' lives too. This gives us power and strength to work for good.

PONDER

How can I find ways to practice faith, hope, and love more deeply in my daily life?

PRAY

God of hope, strengthen my faith that I may trust in hope and better love all who cross my path.

15 | WHEN ALL SEEMS DARK

*Jesus firmly tells us not to be afraid of the upheavals
in every period of history, not even in the face
of the most serious trials and injustices.*

When things are going well it's easy to believe in
hope. But when situations are beyond our power to
control or affect, our human tendency is to throw
up our hands and retreat. On the contrary, as Pope
Francis clearly stated at the closing of the Jubilee
Year of Mercy, when we place our hope in Jesus, he
will not leave us abandoned. Even in the midst of
trials, we can rely on God's goodness and attention.
The smallest actions done in hope and trust (even if
we may be acting "as if") make a difference. Hope
is the key.

PONDER
How can I increase hope in the dark times as well
as in the light?

PRAY
God of hope, remind me that you are always with me!

16 | GOD IS ALWAYS FAITHFUL

*Before God asks anything of us he makes
us a promise. Even Adam exiled from Paradise
left with a promise.*

"Hope does not disappoint" (Romans 5:5). Pope Francis repeats this sentence over and over in homilies and other addresses that he has made all over the world since his election in 2013. "This is our destiny," he says, "always to walk in confidence of the promises." And there's the word it's so important to remember in our insecurities and uncertainties: *confidence*—the fundamental principle of the virtue of hope. This takes work on our part—ironically, we may have to suspend our belief in what we see in order to see *in faith* that God's promises are real. But when we are able to do that, our confidence is multiplied, and we are able to hope with great joy.

PONDER

Is "confidence" an active word in my vocabulary?

PRAY

God of hope, help me trust beyond what the world tells me so that I may share your good news!

17 | THE FULFILLMENT OF A MYSTERY

*The Church must keep the lamp of hope burning
and clearly visible, so that it may continue
to shine as a sure sign of salvation.*

Pope Francis is fond of reminding us that Jesus came to re-create us, to foster the hope in us that life with God begins now, in how we live our lives. And Jesus was a fearless model of God's love in all that he did and taught. We are the church Pope Francis speaks of—we are called to keep that lamp of hope bright and shining. In our work with the poor and voiceless, in our care for the sick and dying and young and helpless, in our love for all people, whatever their situation, nationality, or religious belief, we carry this light, acting as beacons of hope in a dark world so that others may be led by God's light.

PONDER

How brightly does my light of hope shine?

PRAY

God of hope, infuse my darkness with your light of hope, that I may be light for others.

18 | WHERE DO WE FIND HOPE IN THE WORLD?

*I cannot give you hope, but I can tell you
that hope is where Jesus is.*

Pope Francis recognizes that we, being fallible human beings, ask for signs, looking for proof (just like the apostle Thomas) that hope is a realistic virtue to hold. So he points out that hope is where Jesus is, and Jesus is everywhere. When our own hope is dim, perhaps there are loved ones, Facebook friends, coworkers, or the server who refills our coffee cup who model hope and quiet joy. There are people working for justice and peace and a livable planet for coming generations who are trying to make people's lives better in the face of daunting odds. If they can carry on in hope, mightn't we try to emulate them and their confidence that God's presence is alive and well in our world?

PONDER

Where will I see evidence of God's goodness today?

PRAY

God of hope, open my eyes that I may see you!

19 | TRUST BEGINS NOW

*We must always rely on the Lord, in life's little things
and also in the big problems, so that trusting the
Lord becomes a habit.*

Turning our lives over to the care of God is a struggle. We often think we know better than God how things should be arranged, what will make us happy. Pope Francis says we must keep our focus on God and how God is already working in our lives and in our world. When people in 12-step programs begin to take recovery seriously, healthy new life habits take the place of old, destructive ones. In the same way, Pope Francis reminds us, making trust in the Lord a habit will fill us with the hope we seek. And sharing it with others will help it to grow.

PONDER

What one habit can I put aside so that I can focus better on God?

PRAY

God of hope, help me to trust you always.

20 | LIVING STONES

We have been called to great hope.
Let us go there.

Pope Francis asks us to remember Jesus' words to his apostles about the Advocate to come, the Spirit that would fill their hearts and make them proclaim God's Good News with courage and conviction. Jesus prayed that all may be one—it is this unity of heart and soul that should inform everything we do in hope. We find hope in ourselves, we seek it in others, and together we help it to take root and make a real difference in our world. And, always, Pope Francis reminds us, we are not alone. The Spirit is always with us, and the Spirit's hope, manifested in others, will uphold us when we are weary.

PONDER
Am I ready to go where God is sending me?

PRAY
God of hope, help me feel your Spirit always guiding me, leading me in your path.

21 | WHEN WEARINESS AND DISILLUSION STRIKE

Have courage! Let nothing rob us of the joy of being the Lord's disciples.

Pope Francis is always a realist when it comes to understanding human nature. He knows that fine words and lofty sentiments will not feed a soul that is caught in the web of the world's injustices, violence, and dread. He knows that hope can be hard to come by in these times. But keeping our focus on the fact that we are never abandoned by Jesus is a way to keep forging ahead. He says, "Let us not allow ourselves to be robbed of the hope of living this life together with Jesus and with the strength of his consolation." It helps to have a companion on your journey!

PONDER
Where is the first place I turn when I feel disgusted with life?

PRAY
God of hope, remind me always that you are with me, so that I may have the courage to be hopeful!

22 | SPREADING THE WEALTH

Let us not rob others of hope;
let us become bearers of hope!

At the same time that Pope Francis is urging us not
to lose hope, he also challenges us to share hope
with others. The first and best place we do that
is close by—in our homes, in our parishes, in our
workplaces. When we begin to live in hope and start
working with the joy that hope inspires, we become
more aware of those who need that spark themselves.
What greater way to find hope than to give it to
others! Oscar Hammerstein II once wrote that love
only becomes love when it is given away. The same
could be said for hope: to share it is to make it grow.
And when we live what we proclaim, our own confidence is enriched. It is truly a win-win situation!

PONDER
Can I find someone today who needs to hear a
message of hope? Can I share it with joy?

PRAY
God of hope, keep hope alive within me!

23 | UNITED IN PURPOSE

Our efforts must aim at restoring hope, righting
wrongs, maintaining commitments, and thus
promoting the well-being of individuals
and of peoples. We must move forward together.

When he spoke to the U.S. Congress, Pope Francis spoke bluntly and passionately about our commitment to one another the world over. We are one global community, and what hurts one hurts all. In caring for refugees (and their reasons for fleeing their homelands), in care for the planet (and ensuring that all peoples will have livable environments), we have a clear mandate to live responsibly, and to do so in a way that elevates instead of denigrates others. Hope will give us the courage to take up this task with joy.

PONDER

What are some issues affecting my local community that could use my help?

PRAY

God of hope, open my eyes to the needs of all my brothers and sisters who need your hope!

24 | FINDING OUR FOOTING

*Hope bears us up so we don't drown
in the many difficulties that face us.*

Hope is a "humble virtue," Pope Francis says, and one that needs attention to maintain. It requires hard work on our part, sometimes, to keep hope alive, but Pope Francis insists that it is the primary virtue for inspiring others. Faith may give us the grounding to know that God is real and with us. Love may help us find a way to live the gospel message. It is hope, though, that powers our action, that bolsters our faith, and that strengthens our love. Hope helps us reach out to others, to see us all as united in our common struggles, and it helps us all find the courage and conviction to keep working for the good of all.

PONDER

Which virtue is easiest for me to practice? Which is the hardest?

PRAY

God of hope, increase my trust and hope and joy so that I may always be an effective witness of your goodness!

25 | DO NOT BE AFRAID

*If you have peace of soul in times of darkness,
when everyone is enjoying your pain, that is a sign
that you have the seed of the hopeful joy.*

Pope Francis says that "Do not be afraid!" is the message of the church. It is true that stalwart messengers of hope may be scorned and scoffed at by those who "enjoy your pain," but that is no reason to back off. Instead, it is an additional spur to increase hope and joy, especially in the company of others who are united in making the world a more peace-filled, hope-filled place. Search your soul, Pope Francis says, for that quiet peace that comes from knowing you are surrounded and protected by God's love. That peace is the clearest sign that you are living in hope.

PONDER

How often am I able to sense quiet peace in my heart?

PRAY

God of hope, take away my fear and fill me with conviction!

26 | BLESSED ASSURANCE

Be assured that the Lord never abandons us.

Regardless of our conviction and stoutness of heart, there are bound to be times when our spirit flags and we wonder if spreading the message of hope is becoming empty. This is when we may find ourselves giving in to complaining and self-pity. Pope Francis asks us to be especially aware at these times of resting in the assurance that God is always with us. Just as peering into the deepest darkness can reveal the tiniest pinpoint of light, looking deeply through those moments of discouragement can highlight the hope that is still there in our souls. By remembering that God never abandons us, we open our hearts enough to let hope re-emerge.

PONDER

When I am in times of darkness, do I remember that God is with me?

PRAY

God of hope, keep me mindful of the hope that is sometimes dormant in my soul!

27 | GOD'S MERCY NEVER ENDS

Hope, lying deep in our hearts, is the proof of the power of God's mercy.

When trying to explain God's unconditional love and mercy, Pope Francis frequently turns to the parable of the prodigal son. The image of the father who waits eagerly for a glimpse of the son returning is, for Pope Francis, a model of God's constant presence with and longing for us. The biggest revelation of all is that we needn't go searching outside of ourselves for God's mercy—the hope that we seek is within us always, just waiting to be revealed. All we have to do is ask and look for it. For this reason, Pope Francis reminds us, it is good not to be isolated, but to keep sharing the message with others who are on the same quest. What we may not find alone, we may find together!

PONDER

How deeply within me is hope buried, or do I carry it proudly?

PRAY

God of hope, help me to trust you always!

28 | SILENT, HUMBLE, STRONG

What unites my Christian life to your
Christian life, from one moment to another,
in the darkest moments of life, is hope.

Pope Francis reminds us often that hope thrives in community. Each of us in the church is united to all others in the church. Our lives are bound together by the shared hope of the goodness of God's message—the hope of justice and peace overcoming violence and war, the hope of mercy and dignity and safe living as a realizable human right for all people. This is who we are as the church, and when we work for the good of all, even in our darkest moments, we are infused by the light of hope to carry on. Hope, Pope Francis says, is "silent, humble, but strong." Let us trust in this good news!

PONDER

How often do I remember that I am connected with all Catholics everywhere?

PRAY

God of hope, help me to remember that hope is never wasted but is an essential part of your goodness!

29 | BECOMING PEOPLE OF HOPE

A Christian is a man or woman of hope who knows that the Lord is present and who finds peace and joy through working for the good of others.

Being people of hope means that we must continually nourish that hope within ourselves by the help of others, always focusing on God's nearness and promise of goodness to come. Pope Francis stresses the importance of always including others in our hope, of treating one another as equal creations of the God who loves us, of overcoming conflict and enmity through the force of the hope that unites us. Some days this will be easier than others, yes, but it's always important to keep on trying. We can inspire others with our hope, and they can inspire us!

PONDER
Where in my life do I most need to "grow" hope?

PRAY
God of hope, help me to remember the holiness of others and to love others as you love me.

30 | GET IN THE GAME!

*Today, accept reality and carry it forward,
make it bear fruit, render it fruitful.*

When the world is divided by conflict, when people live in terror, when insecurities are rampant, talk of hope can seem like a fairy tale. Not true, says Pope Francis. Talking of hope and living in hope in the midst of reality are what will carry the message forward. This is our call—to respond in hope wherever we find ourselves, with our eyes and hearts open to bringing hope vividly and enthusiastically to those who need it most. God is calling us to be fruitful, Pope Francis tells us. "God calls you to pass this life on. God calls you to create hope. God calls you to receive mercy and to give mercy. God calls you to be happy. Do not fear! Do not be afraid! Get in the game!" May hope be our guiding force always and in all ways!

PONDER

What first hope-filled step will I take today?

PRAY

God of hope, fill me with your light and grace!